Beautiful Angels of Mine

Written By Frances Ruocco

Illustrated by Mira Kheyman

Copyright © 2023 Frances Ruocco

All rights reserved. No part of this publication may be reproduced, distributed, or transmitted in any form or by any means, including photocopying, recording, or other electronic or mechanical methods, without the prior written permission of the publisher, except in the case of brief quotations embodied in critical reviews and certain other noncommercial uses permitted by copyright law.

ISBN: (E-Book) 978-0-9743366-3-3
ISBN: (Paperback) 978-0-9743366-4-0
ISBN: (Hardback) 978-0-9743366-5-7

Any references to historical events, real people, or real places are used fictitiously. Names, characters, and places are products of the author's imagination.

Frances Ruocco

Acknowledgements

As always, I wish to thank the Blessed Trinity, our Lady, for all blessings received, as well as my guardian angels, who constantly watch over me. Secondly, I wish to thank God for my six children, ten grandchildren, and one great-grandchild, who will always hold special places in my heart. Last but not least, all family members and friends who always support me in all I do. A special thank you to Mira Kheyman for her artwork. I am sure you agree that she is a very talented artist.

I pray that everyone reading this book believes that God sends us as many guardian angels as we need to guide and protect us on our journey back home to Heaven.

Amanda and the other angel children were in the auditorium practicing their songs and dances for this year's Christmas celebration. Many angel children would perform in the play, and each one anticipated being the special angel chosen for one of the starring roles.

Some angel children wrote songs; others will be dancing; still others were part of the various groups who decorated, cleaned, or helped serve food. Every job was very important to the success of the party. On December 8th, Dominic's song "Beautiful Angels of Mine" was picked by God as the winning song.

The following week, on December 15th, they picked Amanda to sing his song at the celebration on Christmas Eve. As always, there was a lot of excitement, and the angel children had enjoyed themselves during the past two weeks. Angel Taylor, whom the angel children called Miss Taylor, was directing the play. She was a beautiful adult angel with eyes as blue as the sky and long, dark brown hair.

Angel Nicole would be playing the chimes, and Angel Charlie was going to play the piano. They had learned to play the instruments so that when they lived on Earth, they would play at various schools and teach Earth children how important music was in all of our lives. Amanda and the other angel children loved learning all the new songs that God would inspire the Earthlings to write.

Miss Taylor knew songs for every season of the year, especially all of the holidays. From time to time, Miss Taylor would tell the angel children stories about Earth children. Stories about how they loved singing nursery rhymes, dancing, playing tag, baseball, football, bowling, and many other games.

Amanda and the other angel children thought these stories sounded just like the fun things they did in Heaven. Hearing the stories about the Earth children playing the same games gave them a special kinship with the Earth children.

Of course, Earth's children could not float around or jump from cloud to cloud. In fact, Miss Taylor told them about one Earth child who tried to jump down seven steps and landed in such a way that he broke his arm. She said it happened all the time on Earth.

Things like that never happened to Amanda or the other angel children in Heaven. Why they could jump from one star to another, sometimes even five stars away, and if they missed one star, they could just float around until they came to the next star, or they could float to whichever star they wanted, even if it was one hundred feet away.

When the Earthlings first started sending their rockets up into the sky, a lot of the angel children were frightened because they thought that the strange shapes would hurt them and stop them from still being able to jump from star to star. However, they soon realized that although the angel children could see the earthlings, the earthlings could not see the angel children, and the rockets would pass right through them without doing any damage. Amanda and the other angels did not like the noise or dirt the rockets left behind. They also thought that God spoiled the earthlings, why they would never get away with making such a mess in Heaven.

Nevertheless, it was interesting to watch the earthlings float in the sky. They looked so uncomfortable in the outfits they wore, and they could never have the freedom that the angels had. In fact, the angels soon realized that the robes that the angels wore were much lighter and the earthlings looked warm and

confining. They were thankful they did not have to wear those icky outfits.

Angels Sal, Charlie, and Joey loved the fact that the angels were faster and could breathe without any machines. All the angels knew they were much happier flying around the sky than the earthlings could ever be. However, there were times when they loved to watch the faces of the earthlings for hours. The angels could see how the earthlings faces changed from being afraid to wearing big smiles as they looked at all the beautiful colors, shapes, and shooting stars they saw in the sky.

There were other times when Miss Taylor would let the angel children look through the looking glass and watch Earth children at play. Sometimes, they would see countries where Earth children had no food or were very sick. That always made the angel children sad, and they wished they could do more to help the Earth children.

Amanda and other angel children wondered why the adult Earthlings spent so much money going into space, instead of helping these sick Earth children, but some Earthlings believed they learned from being in space.

Amanda hoped that was true, but if it wasn't, she wished the Earthlings would realize there wasn't any other life in space and use the money to help the poor children on Earth.

Some of the older teenage angels, like Toni Ann, John, Paul, Alexandra, and Victoria, as well as many adult angels, were allowed to fly down to Earth and become guardian angels for the Earthlings. Of course, all angels knew that wasn't always an easy job because there were many temptations on Earth.

Actually, everyone knew the guardian angels could send signals back to Heaven asking for extra help. What the Earthlings did not know was that each time a guardian angel had to get extra help from Heaven, it put him or her in jeopardy of not keeping his or her wings.

Why, some of them might even have their wings taken away for a long, long time. Then that guardian angel would have to return to Heaven for refresher courses and when sent back to Earth, might not be given the same earthling that had been originally assigned to that guardian angel.

The earthling and his or her new guardian angel would then have to start all over again. Even though things eventually worked out, it was such a waste of time. In addition, earthlings don't always feel as comfortable with their new guardian angels as they were with the guardian angel, they had for so many years of their lives. It was as bad as being left back in school and having to make all new friends or having your best friend move away from you. Most humans are not happy when that happens; in fact, even angels do not like to lose their angel or earthling friends. Amanda wished all earthlings were good so that all the guardian angels could get their wings and keep them forever.

The yearly party was always very special because everyone in Heaven celebrated the birthday of Jesus, and many of the angels received not only their wings, but also special recognition at the celebration.

Angels were always prepared to help Earthlings perform special works and/or change their Earthly bad habits to Heavenly good habits, but the angels had to be asked for that help. Guardian angels were never allowed to interfere in any problems if the Earthlings did not ask for help.

Angel Taylor was reviewing everything and taking notes. There appeared to be only a few final touchups to be done in preparation for the party.

The singing angel children were practicing all the new songs that have never been heard on Earth yet and the dancing angel children were practicing their routines one last time before the final performance. They looked better than any group of dancers on Earth.

The costumes were finished, and all neatly hung on the rack waiting for the angel children to wear in the play. The female angels were wearing either sparkling cherry or deep hunter green gowns. The male angels were wearing the deepest royal blue suits with light shirts.

Some outfits were made from the softest velvet; others were made out of satin. There was also a new fabric that had never been used on earth before. Why the angels hadn't even picked a name for it yet. Everyone had heard about the new fabric and color, but no one was allowed to see it yet.

Alexa and Matthew were checking that all the background settings were painted sparkling bright colors; and every stage angel was ready and anxiously waiting just as the workers did at every Broadway play on Earth.

Groups of teenage angels were helping the adult angels prepare the food. There were meat and vegetable dishes, cookies, candies, ice cream and cakes for the party. Angel Brendan was hanging around the kitchen in case there were any samples of all the goodies. He had never seen so many different goodies in his life. Every time he went near one of the tables, an adult angel went tsk, tsk and shook her finger at him.

Everyone was having fun helping each other and the adult angels always sang songs while they were working. They sang songs from the old days and loved to retell tales about the events that took place at their celebrations hundreds of years ago.

Amanda had not stopped worrying since she was chosen to sing the solo in the play.

The closer the hands of the clock neared midnight, the more she got a queasy feeling in her stomach and her hands began to shake.

Miss Taylor told her to remember three important lessons.

First, you are not the only angel child feeling that way;

Second, once she started to sing, the words would flow naturally, and she would be fine; and

Third, her beautiful voice was a gift from God and the best way to thank God for that gift was to share it with others.

Amanda was dressed in a light lilac gown. On her head, she wore a flower piece of lilacs and baby breath, which cascaded down her back entwined with dark purple ribbons. She peeked through the curtain and looked straight ahead, then from one side of the auditorium to the other side and up into the sky. She drew in a deep breath and whispered: "Oh, my."

There were more angels than she had ever seen in her life. In fact, she never knew so many angels existed, why there were angels floating wing to wing and on every cloud. Amanda thought she was going to faint.

Miss Taylor came over to her and said, "Take a deep breath Amanda, stay calm, everything will be all right."

"I can't do it," whispered Amanda as tears filled her eyes.

"Yes, you can," Miss Taylor said, "Remember what I told you about thanking God for the beautiful gift He gave you". "You will be saying thank you to God with every note you sing, and everything will be fine."

Where did they all come from?" asked Amanda.

Miss Taylor said, "You know that this is one of the brightest and happiest nights in Heaven Amanda, so all of the angels try and drop in, if only for a little while. Don't panic, everything will be fine and afterwards it will become one of the greatest memories of our lives."

Amanda just stared - she was speechless.

Trust me Amanda, I have worked with gifted children for many years on Earth and I never heard a voice as beautiful or pure as yours. You put all the love you have for God into this song and it can be heard in every note you sing. God has truly blessed you and He would not want you to waste that talent."

Miss Taylor knew that some of the angels had heard Amanda practicing and were so delighted with what they heard, that they told their friends, who told their friends, who told their friends and so on, but Miss Taylor would not mention that to Amanda now.

It was true that all the angels from Earth stopped in to wish Jesus a happy birthday and find out which angels got their wings and recognition for a job well done. However, this year they were all trying to be here at the same time to hear Amanda sing.

God protect Earth without any angels there to keep Earthlings on track, thought Miss Taylor. The fallen angels could have a field day creating havoc down there.

Miss Taylor looked at Amanda and whispered, "This is it."

Amanda felt her throat go dry. She took a quick sip of water, the curtains opened as angel Charlie began to play the piano. As soon as Amanda heard the first note, she forgot about how frightened she was. Instead, she thought about how much she loved God; how much she loves to sing; how lucky she was to be given such a beautiful voice; and the words just emerged as pure and beautiful as they always had, filled with love and devotion.

Beautiful Angels of Mine

"Beautiful Angels of mine, your job was sublime
Through all of the snares, through all of your fears
You didn't retreat, never accepted defeat
As I watched you on Earth, I was proud of your work
Never leaving their side, just trying to guide
Earthlings who seemed lost, unaware of the cost
You led them back home to my Heavenly throne
Your praises I sing, forever earning your wings
Notice their eyes how they shine, your work was sublime
As you fly through the sky, you will attract every eye
Known throughout all time, as Beautiful Angels of Mine.'

The angels were speechless, their eyes lit up and each one held their breath in wonder. Everyone was so overwhelmed that no one clapped.

Amanda thought they were not pleased with her singing and turned to walk away.

Suddenly the applause began, the angels yelled "bravo, bravo," "magnificent," "beautiful." Tears began to run down Amanda's face, tears of relief, tears of happiness and tears of love.

The next day, when the angel children were remembering the previous night's happenings, they asked how the Earthlings had survived without all the angels there to help protect them.'

Miss Taylor said: "An amazing thing happened on Earth! Many of the Earthlings were busy celebrating Christmas themselves, many were at Mass, while others were with family and friends and in a very loving and giving mood."

The naughty angels had heard so much about Amanda's voice and they were so curious about it themselves, that they forgot about the opportunity they had to do so much damage. In fact, many of them decided to change sides. We are all hoping that the seeds will stay firmly planted and they will stay with us forever and never change their minds and leave us again.

The leader of the fallen angels was extremely angry at first, but even he had to admit that Amanda's voice was magnificent and there would always be other days to come when he could practice his devious deeds. After all everyone knows, we win some and lose some every day.

Miss Taylor said: "Who knows, maybe some of the naughty ones are getting mellow in their old age, maybe they are tired of fighting and want to call a truce and try for peace again. Maybe they miss being home."

Amanda smiled, maybe Miss Taylor was right, just as she was right about last night being a night she would never forget as long as she remained in Heaven, and yes, Amanda knew that she could share that night with her loved ones for generations to come.

Draw Some Angels Decorating a Christmas Tree and a Birthday Cake for Jesus. What Gifts Would You Give to Him?

A Puzzle For You. Can You Find the Words? Have Fun.

```
              *
              M
             SEE
            CAROL
           GETRAIN
          EARYHITE
         BCHRISTMAST
        SETTHHBOOKSY
       LEHAPPYNEWYEAR
      LPRANCERIORLICWAN
     WISHOESLISTTMDOLLSY
        BABYTTMJESUS
            PMO
            CAR
            ASM
            CPT
```

We want to WISH you a MERRY CHRISTMAS and a HAPPY NEW YEAR. Look for PRANCER by the North STAR. Don't forget to sing a CAROL or two. We have many DOLLS, although so many children have also asked for BOOKS; CAR and TRAIN on their LIST. I hope that we will make all children happy. Most important of all find BABY JESUS the reason we celebrate Christmas. Draw some toys under the tree.

Draw What You Think Some of the Angels Look Like.

MUSIC

Music is such a lovely sound,
always near and always around.
You hear it every single day,
a part of our lives in every way.
In the evening crickets rubbing their feet,
in the morning birds singing so sweet,
As the wind blows through the trees,
at home or office from computer keys.
From the tiny lips of babies who coo,
or two lovers whispering, "I love you!"
So many sounds, such different beats,
adding to life's extra special treats;
Heard at the opera and the ballet,
a symphony concert or a Broadway Play

Movies, TV, radio and who could forget
school and backyard plays with our own set.
When at a dance or a special affair,
how happy we are that music is there.
Dancing, clapping, and singing lines,
giving to people such happy times.
It cheers a heart, clears a mind
of any problems had at that time,
Loved by young and old as well,
don't you agree music is swell?
And what a gloomy world this would be,
without music giving pleasure to you and me.

Written by: Frances Ruocco
Illustrated by: Mira Kheyman

Can You Write Jesus a Happy Birthday Poem?

www.ingramcontent.com/pod-product-compliance
Lightning Source LLC
Chambersburg PA
CBHW042146290426